WOMEN & IDENTITY

9 STUDIES FOR INDIVIDUALS OR GROUPS

Adele Ahlberg Calhoun & Tracey Bianchi

With Notes for Leaders

IVP Connect

An imprint of InterVarsity Press
Downers Grove, Illinois

InterVarsity Press
P.O. Box 1400, Downers Grove, IL 60515-1426
www.ivpress.com
email@ivpress.com

InterVarsity Press® is the book-publishing division of InterVarsity Christian Fellowship/USA®, a movement of students and faculty active on campus at hundreds of universities, colleges and schools of nursing in the United States of America, and a member movement of the International Fellowship of Evangelical Students. For information about local and regional activities, visit intervarsity.org.

LifeGuide® is a registered trademark of InterVarsity Christian Fellowship.

Cover image: © JenniferPhotographyImaging/iStockphoto

ISBN 978-0-8308-3108-1 (print)
ISBN 978-0-8308-6426-3 (digital)

Printed in the United States of America ∞

g **green**
press
INITIATIVE

As a member of the Green Press Initiative, InterVarsity Press is committed to protecting the environment and to the responsible use of natural resources. To learn more, visit greenpressinitiative.org.

P	20	19	18	17	16	15	14	13	12	11	10	9	8	7	6	5	4	3	2	1
Y	31	30	29	28	27	26	25	24	23	22	21	20	19	18	17	16	15				

Contents

Getting the Most Out of *Women & Identity*

It is a common myth that the average human harnesses only a small percentage (10%) of their brain's capacity. It is, however, no myth that most of us harness only a small percentage of the love, joy and peace that God can give. Ask a woman about love and you are likely to hear about heartbreak. Ask about her friends and you might hear about loneliness. Ask about her own needs and you will hear about the needs of others. Ask about calling and you will hear uncertainty. Ask about her identity, and shame and frustration leak out. Ask about rest and enjoyment, and you will hear laments about time and busyness. We live a small fraction of the life God has for us.

Wholehearted living seems to escape us. Our lives get myopic, circling the minute-by-minute disappointments and demands of the present moment while God whispers softly or at times hollers for us to harness our whole hearts. The Bible stories in this study follow the journeys of women who move through limited places and times in history. Yet, they live fully by embracing God's view that they have the strength and wisdom to live whole lives.

Have you ever been in the presence of a woman who, in spite of hardship, sorrow and disappointment laughs generously, lives freely, and loves God and others sincerely? She lives with grace when a moment goes awry. She is vulnerable enough to own her mistakes, and has courage to tell her story without spin or censorship. She knows how to receive and accept herself as well as those around her. She is animated by purpose and the confidence that she has something of

God to offer this world. She lives her full life. Our desire is that this would happen for you in the midst of your circumstances. Does this sound challenging or perhaps impossible?

If so, you are in the company of women such as Sarai, Ruth, Hagar, Naomi, Hannah, and Puah and Shiphrah, who learned in the crucible of hardships that God's invitation to them was to live wholehearted lives. They maneuvered their way through challenges such as slavery, infertility, gendercide, polygamy, death and poverty, and found God never forgot them. This study features many Old Testament narratives that point to the wholehearted life that comes through Jesus. Ruth and Naomi lay down their lives for one another. Shiphrah and Puah have a Christlike wisdom that enables them to stand up for truth. Mary and Elizabeth set aside their personal comfort and agenda and lean into God's will, just as Jesus did. These vignettes accompany studies that address some of the cultural milieu women face today.

We believe these biblical women have something to teach us today, and it is our hope that by spending time with them you will see yourself and God through new eyes, and that you will embrace what it is to live wholeheartedly.

Suggestions for Individual Study

1. As you begin each study, pray that God will speak to you through his Word.

2. Read the introduction to the study and respond to the personal reflection question or exercise. This is designed to help you focus on God and on the theme of the study.

3. Each study deals with a particular passage so that you can delve into the author's meaning in that context. Read and reread the passage to be studied. The questions are written using the language of the New International Version, so you may wish to use that version of the Bible. The New Revised Standard Version is also recommended.

4. This is an inductive Bible study, designed to help you discover for yourself what Scripture is saying. The study includes three types of questions. Observation questions ask about the basic facts: who, what, when, where and how. Interpretation questions delve into the meaning of the passage. Application questions help you discover the implications of the text for growing in Christ. These three keys unlock the treasures of Scripture.

Write your answers to the questions in the spaces provided or in a personal journal. Writing can bring clarity and deeper understanding of yourself and of God's Word.

5. It might be good to have a Bible dictionary handy. Use it to look up any unfamiliar words, names or places.

6. Use the prayer suggestion to guide you in thanking God for what you have learned and to pray about the applications that have come to mind.

7. You may want to go on to the suggestion under "Now or Later," or you may want to use that idea for your next study.

Suggestions for Members of a Group Study

1. Come to the study prepared. Follow the suggestions for individual study mentioned above. You will find that careful preparation will greatly enrich your time spent in group discussion.

2. Be willing to participate in the discussion. The leader of your group will not be lecturing. Instead, he or she will be encouraging the members of the group to discuss what they have learned. The leader will be asking the questions that are found in this guide.

3. Stick to the topic being discussed. Your answers should be based on the verses that are the focus of the discussion and not on outside authorities such as commentaries or speakers. These studies focus on a particular passage of Scripture. Only rarely should you refer to other portions of the Bible. This allows for everyone to participate in in-depth study on equal ground.

4. Be sensitive to the other members of the group. Listen attentively when they describe what they have learned. You may be surprised by their insights! Each question assumes a variety of answers. Many questions do not have "right" answers, particularly questions that aim at meaning or application. Instead the questions push us to explore the passage more thoroughly.

When possible, link what you say to the comments of others. Also, be affirming whenever you can. This will encourage some of the more hesitant members of the group to participate.

5. Be careful not to dominate the discussion. We are sometimes so eager to express our thoughts that we leave too little opportunity for others to respond. By all means participate! But allow others to also.

6. Expect God to teach you through the passage being discussed and through the other members of the group. Pray that you will have an enjoyable and profitable time together, but also that as a result of the study you will find ways that you can take action individually and/or as a group.

7. Remember that anything said in the group is considered confidential and should not be discussed outside the group unless specific permission is given to do so.

8. If you are the group leader, you will find additional suggestions at the back of the guide.

1

Wholehearted Living

Romans 12

Often we lament that life feels fractured or broken. It seems a bit lacking compared to the images portrayed in our culture or the life we imagine our neighbors have. Airbrushed images of success—like the perfect career, body, family, boyfriend or husband, or home—can make us feel empty or isolated, somehow less than full. Romans 12 debunks the myth that life can be found through achieving, accumulating and aspiring. Paul invites us toward a transformed life in the presence of a God worthy of our love and devotion.

GROUP DISCUSSION. When you flip through the magazines in a doctor's office, what messages do the images, articles and covers convey about life and what it is to be a woman? What is one thing you believe is important about being female that is missing from most magazines?

PERSONAL REFLECTION. While culture has us believe that anything is achievable, how does God intend us to actually live within real limits (age, life stage, resources, time, talents, etc.)? What can God do within these limits?

Romans 12 is a straightforward passage offering a specific to-do list that moves us from fast-paced distraction to a life integrated around love, community, hospitality, prayer and worship. *Read Romans 12.*

1. In this chapter, what does Paul prescribe as an antidote to fragmented, frantic living and loneliness?

Let God transform you by changing the way you think so you'll know God's will for you which is good, pleasing and perfect

2. Paul invites us in verse 3 is to think of ourselves realistically as limited people who need one another. Why does Paul link body imagery to the discussion about transformation (vv. 4-5)?

as body works under direction of the brain, Christians should work together under the direction of Jesus

3. Look at the gift list from verses 6-8. As you read over that list, which gift do you sense is yours?

serving others - refresh
pray

4. How would the gifts that Paul lists build up the community or individuals?

we would gain satisfaction knowing we are pleasing God

5. What keeps you from living into your God-given gifts?

Pre occupied with my own needs

6. In verses 9-13, Paul gives us a list of kingdom work that cannot be accomplished without love and our full presence to God and others.

Where is it difficult for you to sacrifice what it takes to be "joyful in hope," "patient in affliction," "faithful in prayer"?

Requires concentration & effort

---

7. Do you view serving others as a way of life or as an interruption to the life you are living?

as a way of life

---

8. What do verses 9-21 tell us about the life of serving others?

Be genuine - don't just pretend - serve the Lord. Bless persecutors. Don't think you know it all

---

9. In verse 15, Paul offers an invitation to rejoice and mourn with others. Why is this sometimes difficult to do?

Lack of empathy - we don't have the depth of feeling for others that Christ would want us to have.

---

10. How does the pace of life prevent you from full presence with others in times of joy or sorrow?

We are too busy with our own lives

---

11. What does Paul say to do with those who frustrate us or whom we might seek revenge against?

Don't pay back - Live in peace with everyone "Let God do revenge"

12. What adjustments to your current life come to mind as you imagine yourself in a world that centers on seeking peace and reconciliation with others?

more sincere prayer

---

13. What do you need to change in your life, your schedule and your priorities in order to live into some of Paul's invitations?

spend more time with my Bible

Spend time in prayer listening to God's invitation to live within limits and embrace the gift you are to the body of Christ.

Now or Later

In our "fake it 'til you make it" world, consider what it looks like for your love to be sincere. Practice sincerity in the conversations you have this week by not stretching, exaggerating or hiding what is true about you.

2

Made in God

God created the world 50 percent male and 50 percent female! Our population statistics still remain close to these percentages. The creation narrative in Genesis reveals that Adam was not meant to bear 100 percent of the image of God alone. Being alone was the one thing God declared "not good" (Genesis 2:18). The full expression of God's image is realized in the togetherness of both male and female (Genesis 1:26-27). Men don't bear 80 percent of God's image and women 20 percent, or vice versa. Both genders share the same God-given directives, goodness and agency. Both men and women wear the label "Made in God."

GROUP DISCUSSION. Fold a piece of paper in half. Label one side "Masculine," the other "Feminine." Write down the qualities you identify for each side. What similarities and differences appear on your lists? How does our culture treat the differences between men and women?

PERSONAL REFLECTION. How do culture and being made in God's image shape your understanding of who you are? Talk to God about how it feels to embrace yourself as part of the divine image.

Genesis 1 clearly indicates that men and women together bear the image of God. When one gender struggles, the full image struggles to find expression. For the image of God to be reflected in our world it is essential for both men and women to exercise their God-given gifts, passions and callings. *Read Genesis 1–2.*

---

1. In Genesis 1–2, characteristics of God unfold before us. As you read the chapters, make a list of the characteristics of God you see emerging in this part of the creation narrative.

opposites
day/night   *animals*
water/land   *human beings - reign over all - multiply*

---

2. Some of us may sense that certain characteristics found in God are uniquely male or female. Which images do you place with which gender and why?

God delegates
He is orderly

---

3. How might the men you know relate to these female images of God?

Sensitive
Caring
Compassion

---

4. In Genesis 1:26-31, when God finally creates human beings, what does God say about the man and woman together?

5. In verse 28, God blesses both the man *and* the woman! In your context, how do you see God blessing men and women alike?

Read Hosea 13:8, Isaiah 49:15 and Isaiah 66:13.

6. List the qualities you see God exhibiting in these passages.

7. What do the following images tell us about God?
- a nursing mother (Isaiah 49:15)
- a mother bear protecting her cubs (Hosea 13:8)

8. In Isaiah 66:13, God comforts people like a mother comforts her child. Take a moment to list all the qualities it takes to comfort a person. How do both men and women express these "motherly" qualities?

9. Let the face of a woman with deep spiritual wisdom settle into your mind. Consider the qualities she possesses that most remind you of God. List the female and male images of God represented in her.

10. What qualities of God do you want to be visible in your life?

---

11. There is a great divide around gender issues in the church. How can we be part of the healing of this divide even as we strain to honor the full image of God in both men and women?

Pray to receive the "goodness" of your created being. Thank God for making you you. And where you can't be thankful yet, ask for the grace to see yourself as God sees you.

Now or Later

Make a list of qualities in people that we perhaps stereotype as uniquely male or female. Notice what we say "men do" or "women do" that are really things "God does" in both genders when we allow God to work in our lives.

3

Using Your Voice

1 Samuel 25

Speaking the truth can be a daunting task. Speaking up for what is right is to risk reputation and perhaps the loss of resources or even life itself. Throughout history, women—from Joan of Arc to Malala Yousafzai—risked their lives to speak truth. We keep quiet for many reasons, from past hurts to cultural barriers. Yet Scripture is filled with stories that invite women to speak up and trust that God can use our words and voice for kingdom purposes. In 1 Samuel 25 we find the story of a woman who used her voice for the common good.

GROUP DISCUSSION. Have you ever felt your heart racing with the desire to halt a conversation or an action you did not agree with? Discuss a moment when you were afraid to speak up or where you had the courage to speak your truth. What either bolstered or prevented you from using your voice?

PERSONAL REFLECTION. Many of us are told at a young age to keep quiet. Family, a church, the wider culture or friends may have shushed us without realizing its impact on our lives. What was your own childhood experience like? Were there people who helped you speak up? Were there people who quieted your ideas and dreams?

A woman named Abigail used her voice to act on behalf of her family and wider community. *Read 1 Samuel 25.*

---

1. What do you notice about the situation Abigail finds herself in as you read this passage?

---

2. What sort of man was Nabal, and what limits did his personality place on their household?

---

3. We are told that Abigail had both brains and beauty (v. 3). In a culture that rarely hailed women with intelligence, why do you think her intelligence was noted?

Which—intelligence or appearance—do you feel is most prized in our culture today?

---

4. In verse 14 we read that one of the servants came to Abigail with news of the situation. What qualities do you think made Abigail (and makes other people) approachable?

5. The situation called for instant action, and Abigail had to dig deep and quickly find her voice (vv. 18-31). What does Abigail do in response?

What do you think this was like for her?

_____

6. Abigail took risks in diffusing this situation. What did she stand to lose if her intervention went wrong?

What would she gain if her step in faith to meet David went well?

_____

7. Abigail was married to a violent man in an abusive situation. Is there anything we can learn from her that might help women who struggle with similar situations in their lives?

Abigail had resources - She had trust in God.

8. Look closely at verses 28-30. What does Abigail remind David of?

---

9. How might the opportunity to use your own voice to speak into situations help others remember who God made them to be?

Pray about a situation or injustice that you have noticed and ask God how you might be an agent of change.

Now or Later

Keep a list of situations you were in with others that elevated your heart rate this week. Write down the details (who, what, where) and if you sense your voice and wisdom might have changed or diffused a situation.

Nabel -wealthy ; wife Abigail, sensible
        crude, mean
David - we never stole from your (Nabals) family ; will you share c us
abigail to David - God will make you a leader of Israel.
        David thanked her for keeping him from murder
Nabel was drunk - Abigail told him the next day. He had stroke - d
David married Abigail .

4

24/6 Living

In today's rapid-fire culture it is easy to dismiss the entire idea of Sabbath as an archaic, irrelevant heirloom. Who has time to stop? Seven days a week are still not enough to get things done. We need eight or nine days just to catch up. The Fourth Commandment is the only one that begins with the word *remember*. As life races along at 24/7 pace, we are dangerously close to forgetting the gift that comes with stopping.

GROUP DISCUSSION. Ask each person what she would do if she had an entire day off. Discuss how and why this day would be life-giving and why is it so hard to stop and make it happen.

PERSONAL REFLECTION. When and how do you rest? What goes on inside when you stop achieving, striving and earning?

This study delves into the goodness of Sabbath (*shabbat* in Hebrew), which means to <u>stop</u> or to <u>rest.</u> Sabbath reminds us of who we are when we aren't producing. We are, first and last, people made in the beautiful image of a God who rests. *Read Genesis 2:1-3.*

1. What does Genesis 2:1-3 tell us God did after creating the world?

Rested - declared 7th day holy

2. Why do you think God rested?

Dedicate to the Lord your God, set it apart as holy

Read Exodus 20:8-11.

3. In relation to the other commandments of Exodus 20, what do you notice about the length of this particular commandment?

Longer - more explanation

Why do you think God spent so much time explaining the Sabbath command?

To emphasize the need to stop and be grateful to God for all he had done

4. What do verses 9-11 tell us about the challenges the Israelites faced?

5. What challenges do you personally face in keeping Sabbath?

6. To keep the Sabbath holy, what specifically was Israel not to do?

not do any work

What do you think this freedom allowed people to do on the Sabbath?

*Good deeds
save a life*

---

7. During Jesus' day the Sabbath was bogged down in legalism and included thirty-nine intricate rules of what not do on the Sabbath (read Luke 6:9; Mark 2:27). Does the idea of Sabbath feel life-giving or burdensome to you?

*Sabbath - to meet the needs of people
Life giving*

---

8. How does ignoring Sabbath rest affect our world, our families and culture?

we don't give enough time to worshiping God

---

9. If you were to start living a 24/6 lifestyle where would you begin?

---

10. Create a list of three ideas you might include as part of your Sabbath keeping.

*church
Bible reading + study
more time in prayer*

As a way of praying, slow down and rest in God's presence for ten min-
utes. Resist the compulsion to tell God everything. Imagine arms ready to
hold you; sit quietly to enjoy that space of rest.

Now or Later

Read Psalm 46. In verse 10 God tells us to "be still, and know that I
am God." The Hebrew language here is strong and almost militaris-
tic, as if to say, "Calm down and stop striving! I'm God." What insight
does this psalm offer you when you consider Sabbath keeping?

God is always there to help - provide refuge, security + pea
" rescues - protects
Be still + know that I am God - Psalm 46

Matthew 11:28 to 30

5

Friend or Foe

1 Samuel 1

Women often compete for status, attention, jobs, accolades for their children and even for men. And we live in a culture where competition is celebrated and makes big bucks. Consider "reality" TV shows, where women are pitted against one another for sport (*The Bachelor* or *America's Next Top Model*). Competition can turn potential allies or friends into enemies. The book of 1 Samuel opens with a story about competition between two women in a world where a woman's value, future and perhaps very life was tied to her fertility.

GROUP DISCUSSION. When you meet a woman who appears successful in some way (education, career, appearance, financial status), what is your first response to her success? Do you celebrate her, or do you feel threatened? Perhaps both? Why?

PERSONAL REFLECTION. Your reaction to the perceived success of another person may reveal a place of insecurity. How do stories or longings from your past trigger competitive feelings or reactions with other women?

First Samuel 1 tells the painful story of bullying and competition between two women married to the same husband (this was never

God's design for marriage). Jealousy and pride erodes their solidarity and makes it impossible to rejoice with those who rejoice and weep with those who weep. *Read 1 Samuel 1.*

---

1. Describe the relationships between Elkanah, Peninnah and Hannah.

---

2. How did Hannah handle the competition and bullying of Peninnah (vv. 7-8)?

---

3. If you had been Hannah, how would you have responded to Elkanah's attempt to console her (v. 8)?

---

4. Hannah was desperate and made a deal with God to relinquish the very child she wanted. Has competition (or anything else) in your life made you desperate enough to bargain with God?

---

5. Eli misinterpreted Hannah's fervency and thus made a wrong conclusion about her (vv. 12-14). Hannah used her voice to speak her desire boldly and respectfully to Eli (vv. 15-17). What is the result of using her voice?

6. The story eventually moves away from the competition toward the love and grace of God. What must Hannah's heart have felt like once God blessed her with a child?

---

7. What do you think it was like for Hannah to leave her son to God's service and return home without him?

---

8. Hannah eventually prays, "My mouth boasts over my enemies, for I delight in your deliverance" (1 Samuel 2:1). Is this a jab at Peninnah?

Do you think Elkanah's wives ever end their competition?

---

9. Both Hannah and Peninnah were backed into a complicated situation that set them up as rivals. Do you have a similar situation in which God is asking you to lay down jealousy or pride and receive a sister that is difficult for you to love?

10. How might this story have been different if these women had not viewed each other as competition?

Pray for God to redirect the energy you spend measuring up or comparing yourself to others. Ask God to help you believe that you are good enough, just as you are.

Now or Later

Pay attention to the women you choose to chat with or befriend. Do you feel inadequate or superior in any of your interactions? Consider where those emotions come from.

6

Call the Midwife

Luke 1:26-56

We all have times when we labor through a difficult patch. A midwife is trained to help a woman go through the difficulty of giving birth. In a similar way, we can serve as a spiritual midwife to others as they birth a new thing that God is doing in them. Mary and Elizabeth were cousins and friends separated by age and distance. Both were miraculously pregnant, but their situations were complicated. Elizabeth's husband was mute (Luke 1:20), and Mary's betrothed had to decide if he would even marry her. Elizabeth and Mary turn to one another for support and encouragement when their lives took an unexpected turn and they had to give birth not just to babies but the reality of God's will for them.

GROUP DISCUSSION. Have you ever depended on a friend to get you through a hard season? What did she give you that kept you on the path?

PERSONAL REFLECTION. When have you given the gift of your presence to a friend and served as a midwife as she labored through a tough situation? What was it like for you?

Mary and Elizabeth's relationship models the collaboration, interdependence and solidarity that God can provide in a woman who has our back. *Read Luke 1:26-56.*

1. List in chronological order the events of Mary's life represented in this passage of Scripture.

---

2. The angel of the Lord had appeared to Zechariah with news that infertile Elizabeth would bear a son (Luke 1:11-20). Zechariah did not believe the angel and therefore was struck mute for the duration of the pregnancy. What do you think it was like for Elizabeth to live with a mute husband?

---

3. When Elizabeth and Mary greet each other, what happens (vv. 41-45)?

What emotions are expressed?

---

4. Mary's and Elizabeth's greetings are not so much about each other but about what the Lord is doing in their lives. If we did this with our family and friends, in what ways would it change our interactions with each other?

Praise to God

Elizabeth was already pregnant when Mary became pregnant, Mary went to Elizabeth

5. What sort of conversations do you imagine came out of having a mutually supportive rather than a competitive relationship?

---

6. God's plan for salvation involved women who were willing to risk that God's will for them was good no matter how it diverged from their own agenda. How do you think Mary and Elizabeth's friendship helped them cope with fears or confusion about the call God placed on their lives?

---

7. Verse 56 tells us that Mary stayed with Elizabeth for three months. What are modern parallels to the sort of visit Mary and Elizabeth shared?

---

8. Elizabeth gave birth surrounded by neighbors and friends (vv. 57-58). Mary gave birth away from home and friends (Luke 2:4-7). When have you been alone or surrounded by friends as you labored through a major transition in life?

---

9. Where and how do you see Mary and Elizabeth midwifing one another into a new beginning?

10. Where do you need a friend to stand in solidarity with you as you labor to birth a new beginning?

Spend some time praying about where you need a midwife in your journey or need to be a midwife to a friend in her journey.

Now or Later

Read Mary's song (Luke 1:46-55). As you read, remember her life is turning out very different from the one she expected. Still, she is grateful. Where do the things Mary is grateful for resonate with you? Beside each of her gratitudes list one of your own that comes to mind.

7

Wise Women

Exodus 1:6–2:10

If you've seen Dreamworks's *The Prince of Egypt* or Charlton Heston
in *The Ten Commandments*, you already know Moses is the hero of
Exodus. These films leave out the impact of five brave women who
made Moses' very life possible. These women remain largely un-
known, but they showed astounding wisdom in a no-win situation.
Their status, age and backgrounds vary, yet they come together and
risk their lives to resist infanticide.

GROUP DISCUSSION. Describe a time when you were faced with a decision that felt like you were "caught between a rock and a hard place."
How do you deal with the anxiety and stress that surfaces for you in
these seemingly no-win situations?

PERSONAL REFLECTION. How do you currently listen to God for guid-
ance in the midst of decisions? Can you wait? Do you decide quickly
because it feels less stressful than doing nothing? Do you enlist others
in your process?

Pharaoh felt threatened by too many Hebrew boy babies, whom he
feared would grow up and incite a rebellion. So he demanded that
the Hebrew midwives kill the baby boys. In response, five women
listened to God and did something different. *Read Exodus 1:6–2:10.*

1. What was life like for God's enslaved people?

To help moses, God brought 10 plagues. God delivered Israel from Egypt. Egyptians made Israelites their slaves - brutal slave drivers - forced them to build cities as kings supply centers worked them + out mercy

2. Obviously, Hebrew families were under tremendous stress (Exodus 1:12-16). How might a couple or community feel about a pregnancy?

Feared their boy child might be killed

3. What did Shiphrah and Puah do in the face of Pharaoh's edicts (Exodus 1:17-19)?

allowed the boys to live

Hebrew women are vigorous

Where did they find courage to defy Pharaoh?

They feared God

4. Why did God reward Shiphrah and Puah for their behavior (Exodus 1:20-21)?

He gave them families of their own

5. Why do you think Pharaoh instructs the midwives to let baby girls live (Exodus 1:16)?

He didn't think a woman was strong enough to rule - / overthrow

What does this tell you about the value of women in the ancient world?

They were not thought of as being strong

---

6. When Moses was born, what choices were available to his mother (Jochebed) and his sister (Miriam)?

To destroy him or to save him

What risks were they taking?

The king (of Egypt) might kill them for disobeying

---

7. When have you had to risk that God was on your side when others were not?

Where did you turn for wisdom to help bolster you during that time?

To God - to trusted friends

---

8. Pharaoh's daughter also resisted his policy of infanticide (Exodus 2:5-10). Why might she have stood in solidarity with a slave baby and his sister?

*She felt sorry for him - compassion
She named him Moses because she lifted him out of the water*

9. Where is God inviting you into a risky spot that requires you to rely on the wisdom of God through your community to make the right decision?

How I relate to other people at Marquette

Pray that God will help you make wise, bold decisions. Ask God to give you the strength and the guts to trust that God is working in your decisions.

Now or Later

Make a list of what is life-giving and what is life-thwarting about the decision you are facing (see question 9).

8

Jo 9/7/14

Soul Sisters

Enduring examples of female friendship are lacking in pop culture. Gayle King and Oprah Winfrey represent the hallmark friendship for many women today, but beyond this pair there is not much to note. Films for younger children often feature isolated heroines or princesses without mothers and girlfriends (e.g., Cinderella, Rapunzel, Snow White). Rare is the moment when two female friends make headlines. Is it any wonder that loneliness is cited among women as a top struggle? The book of Ruth is a story that combats loneliness and provides a model of fidelity and friendship in the midst of a harrowing situation.

GROUP DISCUSSION. What examples of friendship are you drawn to in art, history, chick lit, fiction or film? What encourages or disappoints you about these friendships?

PERSONAL REFLECTION. Friendship can be a sensitive topic. Perhaps you have had good friends throughout your life and this conversation enlivens you, or perhaps you struggle with loneliness and you dread the word *friend*. What is your own history of friendships?

It is significant that the Bible has a whole book based on the friendship of two women. Ruth and Naomi make a pledge to stick together, and this friendship shapes their futures and weaves them into God's salvation story. *Read Ruth 1–4.*

---

1. What joys and sorrows have Naomi and Ruth experienced in the past ten years of their lives?

Famine - Emelich died.
The sons married - 10 yrs. later the sons died
Naomi was alone
Lord gave people in Judah good crops
Boaz - wealthy - kind - married Ruth

2. With the death of their husbands and the onset of <u>famine</u>, what kind of decisions face Ruth and her daughters-in-law?

where to find food - heard that people in
Judah had good crops again - so they traveled
to their Naomi's homeland

---

3. Which woman do you identify most with and why?

Ruth - Naomi had been good to her. They
were close to each other → Orpah

---

4. Orpah takes Naomi's advice to leave for a better life. What do you make of Orpah and Ruth's decisions?

They were different personalities. Perhaps
Orpah was being obedient

---

5. Ruth trusted Naomi with her life and risked leaving everything she knew to begin life in a foreign country with an "older" woman. Ruth must have calculated the cost. What might have been the pros and cons of standing by her friend?

She would open herself up to new
opportunities

6. Naomi returns to her homeland without the things that matter
most: husband, children, land. Naomi told her kinfolk to call her
"bitter" (Ruth 1:20-21). What has left you with bitter feelings?

---

7. What did Ruth's friendship with Naomi model to others?

*Loyalty - God blessed her for
her kindness*

---

8. How did God care for Naomi and Ruth as they made their journey
together?

*when they arrived at Bethlehem, the town
was excited about their arrival*

What provisions did they receive, and how does their story end?

*Boaz treated Ruth well - married her
Ruth picked stalks of grain*

---

9. What do we learn about God through the sacrificial love of these
women?

He rewarded them

---

10. How does this narrative foreshadow the way Christ befriends
and extends his sacrificial love to us and through us to others?

Pray that God would strengthen the friendships you have and bring life-giving friends to heal the lonely aches in your heart. Ask God where you might serve as a friend to a woman in need of a companion.

Now or Later

Make a list of the adjectives you would use to describe Ruth and Naomi's friendship. What do you see? How might you live out this sort of adjective list with a woman God has for you to befriend?

strong,
enduring

Famine in Israel - so Boaz Elimelech (from Bethlehem in Judah) took family to live in Moab. wife, Naomi Elimelech died - Naomi to return to Judah & good crops again. Naomi told daughters in law to return to their homelands. Orpah did. Ruth refused

Boaz - rich + influential; Ruth to pick up stalks kind   of grain

Naomi tells Ruth to go lie down ē Boaz family loyalty

Family redeemer didn't marry Ruth - so Boaz did (might endanger his own estate)

Boaz bought the land & married Ruth - had son Obed Jesse ꜜ grandfather of David

9   *Beth.*

Justice for All

Genesis is dotted with heart-wrenching stories of women—Sarah, Lot's daughters, Rebekah, Rachel, Bilhah, Leah, Dinah and Hagar—who suffered injustice. Hagar is the third woman mentioned by name in the Bible and is the only woman, other than Eve, whose encounters with God are recorded in detail. Her story reveals God's heart for justice through a woman with no rights. Nicholas Kristof and Sheryl WuDunn write in *Half the Sky* that "more girls have been killed in the last fifty years, precisely because they were girls, than men were killed in all the battles of the twentieth century." Clearly, justice for women is still a timely topic.

GROUP DISCUSSION. What is your understanding of or experience with issues of violence against women?

PERSONAL REFLECTION. How do discussions about justice for women resonate with you? For some of us, injustice happens under our own roof. Others may feel far removed from this issue that seems to take place thousands of miles away in a culture we cannot relate to.

Hagar lives at a time in history when slave trafficking was common and acceptable. Notice God's concern for Hagar in this story. *Read Genesis 16:1-14; 21:8-20.*

1. What complicates the relationship between Sarai and Hagar (Genesis 16:4-6)?

Why does Sarai turn on Hagar and mistreat her?

---

2. What do you suppose Hagar's relationship with Sarai and Abram was like before she got pregnant?

Bad

---

3. Why does Hagar run when running is anything but safe?

When have you run rather than stayed put to face a hard situation?

---

4. How does the question God asks Hagar in Genesis 16:8 compare with the one God asks Eve in Genesis 3:13?

5. Why would the angel of the Lord tell Hagar to return to Sarai?

What does the angel promise her (Genesis 16:9-12)?

6. Ishmael sounds like the kind of son that can break a mother's heart (Genesis 16:12). In spite of this fact, God protects and defends Hagar. What hope is offered?

7. Scripture points out that Hagar is seen and heard by God in her misery (Genesis 16:13). What does being seen by God mean to women who feel invisible?

8. Sarah demands that Abraham send Hagar and Ishmael away (Genesis 21:8-10). Through this distressing turn of events, God reveals his plan to care for them. What does God provide for Hagar and Ishmael (Genesis 21:19)?

9. God sees those who are abused and acts for their protection and well-being. How might you want to be part of God's rescuing plan for people who are abused and unprotected?

As Hagar did, pour out your heart to the God who sees you, and pray for those who feel invisible, marginalized and unprotected.

Now or Later

List your own Hagar moments—times when you have felt unchosen, unloved, invisible and unprotected. Is there a person you want to talk to about this?

Leader's Notes

Leading a Bible discussion can be an enjoyable and rewarding experience. But it can also be *scary*—especially if you've never done it before. If this is your feeling, you're in good company. When God asked Moses to lead the Israelites out of Egypt, he replied, "O Lord, please send someone else to do it!" (Exodus 4:13). It was the same with Solomon, Jeremiah and Timothy, but God helped these people in spite of their weaknesses, and he will help you as well.

You don't need to be an expert on the Bible or a trained teacher to lead a Bible discussion. The idea behind these inductive studies is that the leader guides group members to discover for themselves what the Bible has to say. This method of learning will allow group members to remember much more of what is said than a lecture would.

These studies are designed to be led easily. As a matter of fact, the flow of questions through the passage from observation to interpretation to application is so natural that you may feel that the studies lead themselves. This study guide is also flexible. You can use it with a variety of groups—student, professional, neighborhood or church groups. Each study takes forty-five to sixty minutes in a group setting.

There are some important facts to know about group dynamics and encouraging discussion. The suggestions listed below should enable you to effectively and enjoyably fulfill your role as leader.

Preparing for the Study

1. Ask God to help you understand and apply the passage in your own life. Unless this happens, you will not be prepared to lead others. Pray too for the various members of the group. Ask God to open your hearts to the message of his Word and motivate you to action.

2. Read the introduction to the entire guide to get an overview of the entire book and the issues that will be explored.

3. As you begin each study, read and reread the assigned Bible passage to familiarize yourself with it.

4. This study guide is based on the New International Version of the Bible. It will help you and the group if you use this translation as the basis for your study and discussion.

5. Carefully work through each question in the study. Spend time in meditation and reflection as you consider how to respond.

6. Write your thoughts and responses in the space provided in the study guide. This will help you to express your understanding of the passage clearly.

7. It might help to have a Bible dictionary handy. Use it to look up any unfamiliar words, names or places. (For additional help on how to study a passage, see chapter five of *How to Lead a LifeGuide Bible Study,* InterVarsity Press.)

8. Consider how you can apply the Scripture to your life. Remember that the group will follow your lead in responding to the studies. They will not go any deeper than you do.

9. Once you have finished your own study of the passage, familiarize yourself with the leader's notes for the study you are leading. These are designed to help you in several ways. First, they tell you the purpose the study guide author had in mind when writing the study. Take time to think through how the study questions work together to accomplish that purpose. Second, the notes provide you with additional background information or suggestions on group dynamics for various questions. This information can be useful when people have difficulty understanding or answering a question. Third, the leader's notes can alert you to potential problems you may encounter during the study.

10. If you wish to remind yourself of anything mentioned in the leader's notes, make a note to yourself below that question in the study.

Leading the Study

1. Begin the study on time. Open with prayer, asking God to help the group to understand and apply the passage.

2. Be sure that everyone in your group has a study guide. Encourage the group to prepare beforehand for each discussion by reading the introduction to the guide and by working through the questions in the study.

3. At the beginning of your first time together, explain that these studies are meant to be discussions, not lectures. Encourage the members of the group to participate. However, do not put pressure on those who may be hesitant to speak during the first few sessions. You may want to suggest the following guidelines to your group.

- Stick to the topic being discussed.
- Your responses should be based on the verses that are the focus of the discussion and not on outside authorities such as commentaries or speakers.
- These studies focus on a particular passage of Scripture. Only rarely should you refer to other portions of the Bible. This allows for everyone to participate in in-depth study on equal ground.
- Anything said in the group is considered confidential and will not be discussed outside the group unless specific permission is given to do so.
- We will listen attentively to each other and provide time for each person present to talk.
- We will pray for each other.

4. Have a group member read the introduction at the beginning of the discussion.

5. Every session begins with a group discussion question. The question or activity is meant to be used before the passage is read. The question introduces the theme of the study and encourages group members to begin to open up. Encourage as many members as possible to participate, and be ready to get the discussion going with your own response.

This section is designed to reveal where our thoughts or feelings need to be transformed by Scripture. That is why it is especially important not to read the passage before the discussion question is asked. The passage will tend to color the honest reactions people would otherwise give because they are, of course, supposed to think the way the Bible does.

You may want to supplement the group discussion question with an icebreaker to help people to get comfortable. See the community section of *Small Group Idea Book* for more ideas.

You also might want to use the personal reflection question with your group. Either allow a time of silence for people to respond individually or discuss it together.

6. Have a group member (or members if the passage is long) read aloud the passage to be studied. Then give people several minutes to read the passage again silently so that they can take it all in.

7. Question 1 will generally be an overview question designed to briefly survey the passage. Encourage the group to look at the whole passage, but try to avoid getting sidetracked by questions or issues that will be addressed later in the study.

8. As you ask the questions, keep in mind that they are designed to be used just as they are written. You may simply read them aloud. Or you may prefer to express them in your own words.

There may be times when it is appropriate to deviate from the study guide. For example, a question may have already been answered. If so, move on to the next question. Or someone may raise an important question not covered in the guide. Take time to discuss it, but try to keep the group from going off on tangents.

9. Avoid answering your own questions. If necessary, repeat or rephrase them until they are clearly understood. Or point out something you read in the leader's notes to clarify the context or meaning. An eager group quickly becomes passive and silent if they think the leader will do most of the talking.

10. Don't be afraid of silence. People may need time to think about the question before formulating their answers.

11. Don't be content with just one answer. Ask, "What do the rest of you think?" or "Anything else?" until several people have given answers to the question.

12. Acknowledge all contributions. Try to be affirming whenever possible. Never reject an answer. If it is clearly off-base, ask, "Which verse led you to that conclusion?" or again, "What do the rest of you think?"

13. Don't expect every answer to be addressed to you, even though this will probably happen at first. As group members become more at ease, they will begin to truly interact with each other. This is one sign of healthy discussion.

14. Don't be afraid of controversy. It can be very stimulating. If you don't resolve an issue completely, don't be frustrated. Move on and keep it in mind for later. A subsequent study may solve the problem.

15. Periodically summarize what the group has said about the passage. This helps to draw together the various ideas mentioned and gives continuity to the study. But don't preach.

16. At the end of the Bible discussion you may want to allow group members a time of quiet to work on an idea under "Now or Later." Then discuss what you experienced. Or you may want to encourage group members to work on these ideas between meetings. Give an opportunity during the session for people to talk about what they are learning.

17. Conclude your time together with conversational prayer, adapting the prayer suggestion at the end of the study to your group. Ask for God's help in following through on the commitments you've made.

18. End on time.

Many more suggestions and helps are found in *How to Lead a Life-Guide Bible Study.*

Components of Small Groups

A healthy small group should do more than study the Bible. There are four components to consider as you structure your time together.

Nurture. Small groups help us to grow in our knowledge and love of God. Bible study is the key to making this happen and is the foundation of your small group.

Community. Small groups are a great place to develop deep friendships with other Christians. Allow time for informal interaction before and after each study. Plan activities and games that will help you get to know each other. Spend time having fun together going on a picnic or cooking dinner together.

Worship and prayer. Your study will be enhanced by spending time praising God together in prayer or song. Pray for each other's needs and keep track of how God is answering prayer in your group. Ask God to help you to apply what you are learning in your study.

Outreach. Reaching out to others can be a practical way of applying what you are learning, and it will keep your group from becoming self-focused. Host a series of evangelistic discussions for your friends or neighbors. Clean up the yard of an elderly friend. Serve at a soup kitchen together, or spend a day working on a Habitat house.

Many more suggestions and helps in each of these areas are found in *Small Group Idea Book.* Information on building a small group can be found in *Small Group Leaders' Handbook* and *The Big Book on Small Groups* (both from InterVarsity Press). Reading through one of these books would be worth your time.

Study 1. Wholehearted Living. Romans 12.

Purpose: To consider God's design for a whole and healthy life.

Group Discussion. Bring a few copies of popular magazines and pass them around. This is an opportunity for women to confess how popular culture makes them feel. If a woman wants the perfect home, how does

Architectural Digest make her feel? If a woman struggles with her physical appearance, how does *Self* make her feel?

Personal Reflection. These questions explore how God's intentions for our thriving differ from the world's idea of the perfect life. Awareness of our limits is a move toward health and wholeness.

Question 1. This question encourages people to look at Paul's prescription for a full life. The list is long. So ask group members what particular verses stand out to them.

Question 2. God is clear that we cannot have or do everything. The point of body imagery is to remind us that no one person can get all of life done on their own. An eye or hand cannot run a marathon without the legs and lungs. See 1 Corinthians 12 for more insight on gifts and unity and diversity in the body.

Question 3. Resist the urge to dismiss the list. It is very common for women to feel as though they cannot name or fully claim their gifts. Women often feel inadequate or unwilling to celebrate their call and giftings. Dare to pick at least one or two that describe you.

Question 4. Love includes practicing joy, patience and faithfulness, which all require time that our culture would rather race through. We are asked to live as sacrifices, to offer our bodies, minds and hearts to the tasks of justice, love and togetherness, and this always takes presence and time. See also Galatians 5:22-23 for the fruits of the Spirit, which is another list of the way God's goodness is found in our lives.

Question 6. Remember it may not be easy to rejoice with someone who has what we want and can't seem to get. Explore where jealousy keeps us from rejoicing. Notice where we may be initially sympathetic but resist a long, messy journey through grief with another person. God calls us to both rejoice and suffer with others.

Question 7. The image of a cooperative, interconnected, participatory, loving and communal world is God's dream for humanity. It is the presence of the shalom of God's kingdom come to earth. God's dream is both already and not yet here. When we live as Paul suggests, we begin to make the presence of Christ real in our circumstances and bring in the kingdom. Look at Revelation 21 for a glimpse of God's future for all humanity.

Now or Later. The Greek word for sincere in Romans 12:9 is *anypokritos*. It means "unfeigned, undisguised." We can be so good at deceiving ourselves. Ask God to help you be sincere.

Study 2. Made in God. Genesis 1–2; Hosea 13:8; Isaiah 49:15; 66:13.
Purpose: To explore God's image and how it is made visible in all humankind so we can embrace the goodness of our created being and be grateful for it.
Group Discussion. People often come to the texts about men and women ready to battle over the validity of their interpretation of Scripture. This makes it hard to listen to one another, to God and to the text. If people in your group have different understandings of these texts, do not judge and injure one another by forgetting to honor the image of God in the other. Jesus' vision of unity was never sameness. It was unity in diversity.
Personal Reflection. This time of silence offers a moment for people to consider how much of their understanding of themselves is cultural and how much is biblical.
Question 2. Historically masculine images of God dominate the Christian landscape. Focusing on the "feminine" image of God can bring new insights about God's nature and our relationship to the divine. Be prepared for people to feel uncomfortable about feminine images of God. Many of us have more familiarity with the masculine side of God. After all, we often speak of God as Father.
Questions 6–8. These questions explore three texts reflecting God's maternal image. They encourage us to wholeheartedly embrace being a woman made in God's image.
Question 9. This question lands our ideas about the image of God in someone we know and helps us explore what the image of God looks like in person! God came to us in the person of Jesus Christ. We see God in people who mirror characteristics of God to us.
Question 11. Invite the women to share one quality of God's image they would like to celebrate or live into in the coming weeks, and have them consider if this falls into a more masculine or feminine category.
Question 12. Read Jesus' prayer for the church in John 17:20-26. How do you honor this prayer for visible unity in diversity when it comes to men and women?

Study 3. Using Your Voice. 1 Samuel 25.
Purpose: To discover the power of using our voice for God's purposes because it is God's gift for us.
Group Discussion. It is essential that every woman in your group feels heard. Work hard to encourage and empower your group members to share their story of action or inaction by helping them remember that

we are all in process and that no one has all the right or perfect answers. Fear of failure and imperfection keeps us from revealing our whole selves.

Personal Reflection. These questions help us dig up some of the places in our past where we have not felt heard. These wounds can follow us for a lifetime. There can be a three-year-old inside us making important decisions. And we need encouragement to do the work that heals our hearts and voices.

Question 2. Contrast the way Abigail is described with the verbiage used to describe her husband, Nabal. His name in Hebrew means "treacherous, surly, foolish."

Question 4. Consider the risk that the servant took by coming straight to Abigail instead of reporting his findings to Nabal. Custom gave women no voice or power, yet Abigail managed to find both in a culture that devalued women. She was brave and ready to act.

Question 5. Domestic violence is part of this story. Nabal's household was held captive by his violent and erratic behavior. At times, speaking up can put a woman in jeopardy. If you or any woman in your group is in an abusive situation, be sure to ask for or offer resources and support. The National Domestic Violence Hotline is found at thehotline.org.

Question 6. Abigail actually risked her life to speak up and go against Nabal's wishes. She faced death at either end of the situation. David could have had her killed as a representative of Nabal's household, while Nabal could have killed her for acting against his wishes to dismiss David. Abigail's act of faith kept David from rash bloodshed, spared the lives of an entire household and defused a volatile situation. Abigail went on to become one of David's wives.

Question 7. Abigail uses her voice for the good of her whole community. She does not speak up for the sake of being heard, being known, being seen. She speaks up to control the damage of two arguing, angry men and the repercussions that come with it. She lays her own life on the line so her family and others can thrive.

Question 8. Abigail reminds David that God has promised him kingship and leadership. She encourages David and also invites him to consider keeping his anger and frustration in check so he doesn't tarnish his reputation or his opportunity to stand ready to receive God's promises.

Question 9. Before you jump in and comment, be sure you understand some of the complexities. Abigail knew the power dynamics and the players. To use our voice wisely means awareness of how power and personality inform a situation. Everyone has triggers. Being aware of them is crucial to speaking well.

Now or Later. By keeping a list of places that simply elevate our heart rate we can begin to consider where we get triggered. How does this trigger inform where we do and don't speak up? It is always best to pray and discern before blurting out words.

Study 4. 24/6 Living. Genesis 2:1-3; Exodus 20:8-11.

Purpose: To consider how God's gift of Sabbath frees us from an earned identity and grounds us in God's spacious rhythms and unchanging love.

Group Discussion. This question gets at how possible it is to intentionally create a lovely day. Try to get at the motivations that keep us too busy to enjoy stopping.

Personal Reflection. Give the participants time to become honest about (1) how their identity is tied into doing, and (2) the rhythms of their life.

Questions 1–2. God is revealing something beautiful in the divine nature. God doesn't rest due to overexhaustion. God's rhythm is reflected not only on day seven but in the goodness that came with each "there was evening, and there was morning—the [first, second, third, etc.] day." Focus on what God's divine rhythm conveys about the limits and purpose of human life.

Question 5. In our busy, tech-savvy culture, we need to encourage one another to use our imagination and consider whether or not technology helps or hinders our Sabbath-keeping practices. At times we can feel enslaved to our devices. It helps to remember we are not victims without choices. We do not have to check email.

Question 6. For a nation of former slaves, Sabbath reminded God's people that they were free from the cracking of the whip and from working 24/7. One day out of seven they could stop! Even in the wilderness they didn't need to collect manna every day (Exodus 16). One day a week they could stop and enjoy life and give thanks to the God who understood both human limits and human possibilities.

Question 7. Matthew 11:28-30 is Jesus' invitation to us to rest.

> Are you tired? Worn out? Burned out on religion? Come to me. Get away with me and you'll recover your life. I'll show you how to take a real rest. Walk with me and work with me—watch how I do it. Learn the unforced rhythms of grace. I won't lay anything heavy

or ill-fitting on you. Keep company with me and you'll learn to live freely and lightly. (Matthew 11:28-30 *The Message*)

Let this invitation reach into the tired places in your heart and body. **Question 8.** The ramifications of keeping Sabbath affect this entire planet—the earth, the animals, the people who work on Sunday and the economic markets. Sabbath slows everything down. It makes us conscious of where our food comes from. It connects to earth and its resources. It makes something besides productivity the bottom line. A 24/6 rhythm can help us live into human, ecological and humanitarian limits. It can change our world.

Question 9. It is fine to start a Sabbath practice with an hour, if that is where you are. God knows the realities of your life. And the truth is, trusting God with some of these realities rather than shouldering them all will free up some space. The following are some wonderful Sabbath resources: *Living the Sabbath* by Norman Wirzba and *24/6: A Prescription for Healthier, Happier Life* by Matthew Sleeth.

Study 5. Friend or Foe? 1 Samuel 1.

Purpose: To stand in solidarity with other women rather than compete against them.

Group Discussion. Some women may be comparing themselves to others in your group. If your group feels safe enough, consider expanding this conversation to ask where women feel competitive, threatened or supported by one another and how this impacts the group experience. If the group isn't ready to talk about any internal competition, ask how competition at work, with siblings, with in-laws or with neighbors affects their relationships.

Personal Reflection. A friend recently changed her email to "lastonepicked." But there were so many variations on that theme that she had to go through a whole host of options to actually find an email that worked. Most of us have some experience of being the "last one picked." This question allows women to reflect on times they felt overlooked, bullied or mistreated. These experiences are not meant to leave us victims but to open us up to God's healing and transforming work. Authenticity around these questions also builds community and solidarity with one another.

Question 1. Since children were a sign of God's blessing, barrenness was often interpreted as a sign of woman's sinfulness. The community looked down on barren women. Husbands often ostracized, ignored or divorced wives who had no children. This reality may not feel much different for women who face infertility today. Still, Hannah was favored over Peninnah, and what woman wants to be second? However, Elkanah doted on Hannah, giving her little bits of extra from time to time. In a polygamous culture it was not uncommon for a wife to undermine the more favored wives (see Genesis 29:16-18, 31 for another sad story where two sisters shared the same husband). Peninnah's response is natural. It hurt that Elkanah favored Hannah. But Peninnah could make Hannah hurt as well. She could flaunt her fertility and her sons. She could make Hannah miserable for not giving Elkanah what every husband wanted—children (especially sons).

Question 2. Peninnah's bullying undid Hannah. Tears, loss of appetite, feelings of inadequacy were just the tip of the iceberg of pain. Furthermore, each year Hannah's loss was exacerbated by the pilgrimage to worship at Shiloh. Peninnah worshiped with a flock of sons while Hannah prayed alone. Invite women to share their own experiences of how they cope when bullied.

Question 3. When someone is in pain the natural tendency is to want to "fix it." We wonder how we can help and make the pain go away. Elkanah cared for Hannah, recognized her misery and wanted her to be happy. The text doesn't say he told Peninnah to "back off." Nor does it say how Hannah responded to his attempts to comfort. The gift of being present with another person in her pain is often the best help we can give. Not fixing. Not advising. Just being with.

Question 4. When desperate, both Abraham and Jacob bargain with God (Genesis 18:16-33; 28:20-22). Isaiah reminds us that God's generosity is not something we have to compete for (Isaiah 55:1). Bargaining is part of the cycle of grief. Recognizing that it is part of a cycle can keep us from getting stuck there. If you find yourself jealous over the good things happening in the life of another woman, one way to get unstuck from hurt is to begin to practice gratitude for what God is giving you.

Question 5. Hannah did not accept Eli's interpretation of her actions. She corrected a priest! Consider this question in light of the study on "Using Your Voice" (study 4).

Question 6. God answers Hannah's prayer in the exact way she asked. This, however, does not mean that bargaining with God is "the" pattern for getting what we want. In fact, this can turn into manipulation. "God, I will do X if you give me Y." Noteworthy in this story is that Hannah received the gift of a son with joy and handed him back to God with gratitude because she had been heard.

Question 7. According to Jewish tradition a child was weaned anywhere from eighteen months to five years. One might wonder if Hannah kept Eli with her as long as possible, for this boy was her badge of honor and her triumph over infertility. But it was Samuel's life that ultimately was of honor to Hannah and God. By the time she handed Samuel to Eli, he was prepared to hear from God himself.

Question 8. Our stories don't get tied up with a bow and "happily ever after." Losses and wounds and joys all make their mark. Feel free to read part of Hannah's prayer in 1 Samuel 2. Note the ways this prayer reflects how she thinks of God and her life.

Question 9. Reinforce how our own stories are found in Scripture. The Bible is not full of perfect people in perfect relationships. It is authentic, and we can find sisters here to help us in our journey.

Question 10. Every story contains choices. And our choices form or deform us. Viewing our stories through the lens of God's goodness can change choices as well as interpretations of our story. But it can take time.

Study 6. Call the Midwife. Luke 1:26-56.

Purpose: To learn from Mary and Elizabeth how to stand with another as they find God under trying circumstances.

Group Discussion. This question uncovers our basic human need to be connected and supported in our journeys. Our individualist culture values going it alone. It is easy to feel inadequate if we ask for help in hard places. We can worry about being judged and struggle with loads too heavy to carry well on our own. God's dream for this world is that we bear with and care for each other when life gets tough.

Personal Reflection. These questions can create awareness of how God has been present to us in the presence of a friend. God is more than willing to come to us through the face of a friend. The themes of labor, birth and burden sharing are a rich part of Luke's narrative. They shed light and understanding on how to stand with another woman in her joy and her pain.

Question 2. Zechariah's muteness could easily have been interpreted as punishment from God. What it really meant had to be difficult for Elizabeth to explain. Furthermore, with Zechariah unable to speak, Elizabeth too was in need of someone to talk to.

Question 3. Elizabeth's baby leaps inside her. And her acceptance of Mary reinforces in Mary's mind God's acceptance of Mary. There are no questions, no judgment. No sense of jealousy or anger about Mary bearing the Messiah instead of her.

Question 4. Elizabeth could have been envious rather than support-ive. Mary could have been proud rather than humble. But both of these women were honest and vulnerable with one another. They showed their feelings and reactions. No doubt they worshiped, prayed and worked together. Their relationship fortified each of them for what was to come.

Question 6. Mary was betrothed and had expectations for how her life would go. The angel's announcement turned Mary's dreams upside down. Her yes to God's will did not mean she had to go it alone. She still needed a midwife/friend to help her face her fears and support her choices.

Question 7. Mary seems to have stayed long enough to visit, help and perhaps even assist at the birth of Elizabeth's baby. Being intentional and consistent through the years in our relationship with a sister can create the same sort of bond Mary and Elizabeth experienced.

Questions 8, 10. These questions invite women to listen deeply to one another's stories—those in the past (question 8) and those they are in the midst of (question 10). Allow stories of the past to create vulnerabil-ity that supports question 10.

Question 9. According to the International Confederation of Midwives, the qualities of a midwife include partnership with another woman, re-spect for human dignity, advocacy, cultural sensitivity and a focus on health and well-being (see "ICM International Definition of Midwife," *International Confederation of Midwives*, internationalmidwives.org/who -we-are/policy-and-practice/icm-international-definition-of-the-midwife).

Question 10. Land the discussion of Mary and Elizabeth's friendship in the current stuff of daily life. Are there practical ways your group can be Mary and Elizabeth to one another?

Study 7. Wise Women. Exodus 1:6–2:10.
Purpose: To understand that God can give any of us wisdom to make the hard decisions that honor God and the well-being of others.

Group Discussion. Some people feel as if they hear from God all the time. Others feel they never do. When we feel that we don't hear from God, it can be tough to make decisions. Hearing from God and choosing wisely is essential part of the Christian journey. We aren't here to decide on our own.

Personal Reflection. Sometimes it is easier to make quick decisions be-cause we don't like the feeling of waiting and "doing nothing." Sometimes we are confident we know best and launch out without considering what God would want or what others might offer by way of advice. Every time we pray the Lord's Prayer we say, "your kingdom come, your will be done, on earth as it is in heaven." The coming of God's will in our life is often accomplished when we as a community listen to God together.

Question 1. Think for a moment about the history of American slavery. What rights did slaves have? The Hebrew people didn't have rights. They were not free to make their own decisions, set their own agendas, develop their own gifts, worship together in community. They were worked to death. In fact, over time Pharaoh demanded that they produce more bricks with less resources (Exodus 5:7).

Question 2. Pharaoh's insecurity around an Israelite workforce that might rebel led him to infanticide. Pregnant women prayed for girls and feared having boys. Mothers were trapped in atrocities like gendercide.

Question 3. Midwives love to see babies born. Shiphrah and Puah found it impossible to turn back on their calling. So they needed to be shrewd in their dealings with Pharaoh. This story came centuries before Psalms, Proverbs and other wisdom literature were written. Still these midwives understood there was a God who loved and created life, a God who valued both men and women, a God who was stronger and more powerful than Pharaoh, a God who would help them. And this informed their decisions.

Question 4. The midwives could have felt God wasn't even in the picture. But God saw and was pleased with their actions. These women valued human life and acted justly, even in the face of death. And God blessed not only them but the people of Israel through them.

Question 5. In ancient times, and in many places today, girls were not valued. They were an extra mouth to feed, useless in war, but useful for menial tasks and sex. Since girls could be controlled, dominated and made to serve, they were allowed to live.

Question 6. They could kill their baby boy, expose him to the environment and let him die, or keep him and expose the whole family to death if Pharaoh found out. With seemingly no room to navigate, Miriam and Jochebed found a way to protect Moses that took risk, creativity, vigilance, passive resistance and bravery (Exodus 2:1-4).

Question 7. These two questions are designed to help women think about current decisions they are facing that seem too difficult for them. It asks them to reflect on their default habits in decision making.

Question 8. Pharaoh's daughter was moved to show compassion when she came upon a crying baby. Perhaps she had not really "seen" with her own eyes what was happening in the lives of the "invisible" life of slaves around her. It is hard not to see a crying baby. In the providence of God, her action led to Moses becoming the man who led the people to freedom.

Question 9. God blessed the midwives, even though they remained slaves, because they listened to God and chose to honor life. These women were also blessed with a deeper awareness of God's presence and the gift of each other in a difficult situation. God also blesses us when we make hard choices. This does not mean that we suddenly win the lottery. Rather, God gifts us with friends, shared stories, greater wisdom and understanding.

If you are interested in learning more about biblical processes for discernment, consider these resources: *Sleeping with Bread* by Dennis Linn, Sheila Fabricant Linn and Matthew Linn; and *Pursuing God's Will Together* by Ruth Haley Barton.

Study 8. Soul Sisters. Ruth 1–4.

Purpose: To see how friendship is one of God's gifts to women for their journey.

Group Discussion. It is important to see that though most women long for friends, our culture rarely supports or portrays substantive relationships between women. The movie industry seems at odds with this. Just check out the Bechdel Test's criteria for movies. The movie has to have at least two named women in it, and the women must talk to one another about something other than a man. According to the Internet Movie Database, not even 2 percent of the movies in the database comply.

Personal Reflection. This question offers time for a woman to honor her own history with friends and the expectations that are in her heart right now.

Question 1. Ruth and Naomi experienced the joy of marriage and the difficulties that come with crosscultural communication. There have been sweet times, tragic deaths, famine and the unenviable position of being a woman without a husband to provide for her.

Question 2. Jewish custom held that when a husband died, his widow stayed with her in-laws. The widow was to wait and hope that either one of her brothers-in-law, a cousin or some other relative would marry her. This custom is the setting for this story. Naomi's husband and sons are dead, leaving her with two young, widowed daughters-in-law, Orpah and Ruth. These three women have no real means of generating income, and the most secure (if not happy) futures for Orpah and Ruth lay in returning home to their families.

Question 3. This question is designed to help women wrap their minds around how all three women respond to the difficulties of life. Orpah plays it safe. Ruth risks. Naomi, an alien in a foreign land struggling with famine, seems to feel that there is no choice for her but to return to Israel, where she might find some friends and family who would care for her.

Question 4. Orpah opts to stay with what she knows and return to her father's family. Perhaps she felt she had more options in Moab than in Israel. Ruth decides she is better off with Naomi. Ruth's words to Naomi (Ruth 1:16-18) are often read at weddings. This pledge to cling, to stay, to hold, to care no matter what happens in the future was originally an exchange between two female friends. Ruth virtually offers to lose her life for Naomi's sake. This tender interchange occurs in a relationship not known for closeness—a woman and her daughter-in-law. To Ruth, Naomi was her mother-in-*love*.

Question 5. *Pros:* Ruth would maintain her tight relationship with Naomi. Moving with Naomi would be a new beginning for Ruth. She would be in a place without famine. Ruth would meet the family of her husband and would gain an understanding his faith. *Cons:* Ruth would always be an outsider and would face crosscultural prejudices and difficulties. And what if something happened to Naomi? Ruth would be far from her own family and country, and would have no guarantees of a future.

Question 6. Old Testament names often represented an experience or character trait. For example, Jacob's name means "holder of the heel" or "supplanter." Leah means "weary" or "tired," and Naomi means "joy" or "bliss," but she changed her name to "Mara" (bitterness) to reflect her struggle. Gently encourage group members to share about when they were (or are) bitter and why.

Question 7. Friendship is a gift—a leaving of myself and a reaching out to the other. Friendship is not just about what I get but what we give. In that way it is a pay-it-forward endeavor. We engage in the tender, compassionate care to benefit our friend, and sometimes that care reaches out to an even broader audience. In a similar way, Jesus calls us "friends" (John 15:15) and models selfless friendship to us. Ruth's fidelity to Naomi resembles the way Jesus cares for us.

Question 8. God provided a kind kinsman in Boaz. God provided space for Ruth to glean. Eventually, God provided a husband for Ruth.

Question 9. Fifty of the eighty-five verses in Ruth are dialogue. The conversations between Ruth and Naomi open us to the gift that comes through sharing our lives with other women. A UCLA study on what happens to a woman's stress levels when she gathers with other women supports the truth that women need one another (see Gale Berkowitz, "UCLA Study on Friendship Among Women," *Chronic Neuroimmune Diseases*, updated January 1, 2014, www.anapsid.org/cnd/gender/tendfend.html).

Question 10. Jesus says in John 15:13 that there is no greater love than "to lay down one's life for one's friend." Ruth laid down her life. And God gave it back to her. Jesus laid his life down to love us. This resurrected Jesus is the truest friend we will ever have, and the model of what friendship can be. Discuss with your group members how they can let Ruth, Naomi and Jesus mentor them in how to be friends.

Study 9. Justice for All. Genesis 16:1-14; 21:8-20.
Purpose: To remind us that God is passionate about justice and concerned for the rights and well-being of women.

Group Discussion. It has not always been clear that women's rights are human rights. Hagar's story creates a context that ties today's slave trafficking and domestic violence to the biblical story.

Personal Reflection. It is easy to center our lives entirely around comforts, opportunities and desires. We love ourselves but not our neighbors. This question invites us to listen to God's heart for this broken world and not just our own.

Question 1. Hagar seems to think that bearing Abraham's baby gives her a special status. This status undermines the relationship between mistress and servant. Sarah uses her authority to strike back at Hagar and remind her of her inferior place.

Question 2. Hagar would have known Sarah (Sarai) better than anyone besides Abraham. Sarah didn't have sisters, family or a mother to talk to. She had slaves. And for Sarah to trust Hagar with her husband speaks volumes about their relationship.

Question 3. In the ancient world all women were vulnerable if they weren't under the protection of a husband, family or tribe. A slave did not belong to herself. She was property, belonging to someone else. Hagar wasn't free to go, and she could not survive on her own with a young son. Running away may have felt like a way to retaliate, but it put them both in danger.

Questions 4–5. God doesn't just give answers. Throughout Scripture God asks questions. Questions can help us understand ourselves. Questions can make us aware of motivations and expectations. Hagar needed to consider the realities of where she could go and what she could do. And unlike Eve, Hagar was honest with God.

Question 7. Hagar was used to being invisible. Her pregnancy suddenly made her feel visible. But it was being seen by God in her misery that sustained her when she had to return.

Question 8. Jealousy and sibling rivalry eventually causes a complete breakdown in the relationship between Hagar, Sarah and their sons. When it is clear that they cannot remain together, God tells Abraham that he has plans not just for Isaac but for Ishmael as well. Imagine what it is like for Hagar to hear that God would make her own son the father of a nation.

Question 9. A couple of good resources regarding injustice and what we might do about it are *Refuse to Do Nothing* by Shayne Moore and Kimberly McOwen Yim, and *Good News About Injustice* by Gary Haugen.

Adele Ahlberg Calhoun has worked in Christian ministry for over forty years. She and her husband, Doug, are co-senior pastors of Redeemer Community Church in Needham, Massachusetts. She was formerly pastor of spiritual formation at Christ Church of Oak Brook, Illinois, and has served as adjunct faculty at Wheaton College. Adele is the author of Spiritual Disciplines Handbook *and* Invitations from God *and coauthor of* True You.

Tracey Bianchi is a freelance writer, speaker and pastor. She serves as pastor for worship and women at Christ Church of Oak Brook where she leads a team that creates contemporary worship each week. She is the author of Mom Connection *and* Green Mama *and coauthor of* True You.

What should we study next?

We have LifeGuides for . . .

Knowing Jesus
Advent of the Savior
Following Jesus
I Am
Abiding in Christ
Jesus' Final Week

Knowing God
Meeting God
God's Comfort
God's Love
The 23rd Psalm
Miracles

Growing in the Spirit
Meeting the Spirit
Fruit of the Spirit
Spiritual Gifts
Spiritual Warfare

Looking at the Trinity
Images of Christ
Images of God
Images of the Spirit

Developing Disciplines
Christian Disciplines
God's Word
Hospitality
The Lord's Prayer
Prayer
Praying the Psalms
Sabbath
Worship

**Deepening
Your Doctrine**
Angels
Christian Beliefs
The Cross
End Times
Good & Evil
Heaven
The Kingdom of God
The Story of Scripture

Seekers
Encountering Jesus
Jesus the Reason
Meeting Jesus

Leaders
Christian Leadership
Integrity
Elijah
Joseph

**Shaping Your
Character**
Christian Character
Decisions
Self-Esteem
Parables
Pleasing God
Woman of God
*Women of the
New Testament*
*Women of the
Old Testament*

**Living Fully
at Every Stage**
Singleness
Marriage
Parenting
*Couples of the
Old Testament*
*Couples of the
New Testament*
*Growing Older
& Wiser*

**Reaching
Our World**
Missions
Evangelism
Four Great Loves
Loving Justice

Living Your Faith
Christian Virtues
Forgiveness

**Growing in
Relationships**
Christian Community
Friendship

Islam → Ishmael
Jewish - Abe - covenant
Christianity -

Nouwen
Henri Nouwen - 1932-1994

"with open Hands"
Ch. 1 to 3

Also by Adele Ahlberg Calhoun
and Tracey Bianchi

True You
978-0-8308-4315-2